THE JOURNEY TO THE SUN

THE
JOURNEY
TO THE
SUN

The Book of Sun Chaser

JOHNATHAN LEVY

Library of Congress Control Number: 2019912212
ISBN: Hardcover   978-1-7960-5379-1
               Softcover   978-1-7960-5378-4
               eBook   978-1-7960-5377-7

Scripture quotations marked KJV are from the Holy Bible, King James Version (Authorized Version). First published in 1611. Quoted from the KJV Classic Reference Bible, Copyright © 1983 by The Zondervan Corporation.

Print information available on the last page.

Rev. date: 08/22/2019

To order additional copies of this book, contact:
Xlibris
1-888-795-4274
www.Xlibris.com
Orders@Xlibris.com
799347

To the little boy who made

it through...keep going!

We must recognize the power of cooperation to build and grow as a people. Yes, we must take control over our own lives and apply ourselves, but we should not have to do it alone. We need to find a way to be able to create with pure intent, flowing freely in our lanes and gifts, allowing everything else to fall in place. Being a human, and helping others to achieve, will help all of us further our own dreams and our collective capacity to grow. We must recognize the positive impact supporting spiritually, mentally, emotionally, and physically can have on the bigger picture. Imagine having the ability to be present in the moment, not being stifled, or limiting the creative flow that exist, but rather embracing and embodying the creative energy and where it is going, allowing for our full expression which would provide greater impact and resonance.

*

Test will always present themselves, many times when we least expect it. We must train our vision to be able to recognize when they appear, understand what is being attempted, how to hold steadfast and find healthy positive outlets to release. So that when we are tested, we will be able to function from a clear space and not one that is repressed or frustrated. We must be mindful to not indulge in entertaining lower negative energy. Ask yourself, is the juice is worth the squeeze?

*

"It's our job to humble ourselves, its Gods job to
elevate us. If we insist on doing Gods job,
He'll do ours."

*

We must be mindful to not press or take too much on, to
not take offence to failed endeavors, controlling what we
can and allowing YHWH to fight those battles that are
not meant for us to engage. Understanding that sometimes
the things we perceive as a slight or loss could in reality be
a steppingstone to elevate or save us. Trust the process,
apply yourself to the task at hand and stay humble.

*

It is not all about me and what I deem to be necessary.
Sometimes it is about being present
and offering support.

*

Life is relative. Where we are is not necessarily where we will
end up. We must be mindful to appreciate where we are, taking
experiences and interactions with a grain of salt, knowing that
there is still room for growth and evolution. Not being so closed
minded or repressed or jaded that it removes the ability and
capacity to love unconditionally and see beyond flaws. Always

being realistic and never naïve. Not a pessimist, but a realistic optimist. We must always allow room.

*

Embrace the progressive energetic flow. Do not
allow distractions the ability or opportunity
to derail that which is known to be true.

*

Appreciate the moments within the moments, that is where life is. That is the present. That is the gift. It is not always about the convenience, or 'best route', or being most pragmatic. It is about the moment and building, the exchange and flow of energy and knowledge and creativity.

*

Do not wait for the perfect storm. When you feel
the inclination, do what you can and continue
to build and grow, showing progression in
the midst. It will never be perfect.

*

Sometimes that which we seek is closer and more
available than we might expect. We must

adjust perspective and expectations in order to
recognize, receive, and utilize. Resources are
readily available to those that show themselves approved.

*

Attention to detail reduces the necessity for repetition.

*

We must not live in the extremes of what we
perceive we can get away with. Justice and
Fortitude at all times in every situation in
every way. Do not cheapen yourself.

*

We must not minimalize even the smallest contribution.
Everything adds up and is invaluable to the process.

*

Accountability and honesty are invaluable forms of currency.

*

We must not over complicate. We must be present
and diligent in action. We must not take
unnecessary liberties. Stick to the script. Stay
true to the task at hand. Prudence,

Temperance, Justice, and Fortitude always.
We never know what is in store.

*

Appreciate the ability to do for others when they cannot do for
themselves. Not occupying negative energy over reciprocation.
Appreciating the ability and the resources to share and
be communal, building relations and letting
love have its perfect place.

*

Understand what is beneficial and do not allowing
over consumption merely for the appeasement
of others. Understanding that it is okay to
engage and socialize while doing so
in a way that does not compromise personal integrity or energy.

*

We must all be mindful and respectful of the
comforts and perspectives of others. Not being
judgmental or pious, but respectful and tolerant,
without the pressure of having to accept.
Being mindful of our dialogue and actions in open settings.

*

Accept that everyone is a different puzzle piece. Appreciate and embrace this uniqueness and its need. Give everyone the ability and their right to grow and discover themselves in their own time and place with correction when warranted, done without judgment.

*

Whatever is meant to be, will be presented at its most opportune time. Patience and appreciation in the midst.

*

There are multiple spectrums at play, and every environment is a micro of the macro. This reality can at times create ill-fated attractions and confusion when similar energies are present. Identifying your spectrum will aide in recognizing what is and what is not for you. Allowing you to avoid non compatible interactions. Allowing you to move with more patience and discernment.

*

Once you have moved past something that is not for you, do not go back seeking it out.

*

Respect opportunities. Do not become complacent
allowing yourself to not be fully engaged
because you do not feel like it.

*

Keep an eye on the big picture. Do not get hung
up on the insignificant. Be proactive in the
approach, execution and follow through.

*

We must recognize and embrace when we possess a higher
frequency energy and the responsibilities that come along with it.
"To whom much is given, much is required." It is better to embrace
the mantle than complain and be stressed every time a situation
requires our assistance.

*

Release old energy and attachments in order
to make room for new connections and
opportunities.

*

We cannot go back and relive life. We must recognize
the mistakes and lessons learned from

our past and apply them to our present and
future. Progress and growth are the goal.

*

Being a lighthouse, means attracting wayward ships.

*

Do not romanticize, wish and or invest energy into
people or situations that are known to be
counterproductive and contrary to our growth,
development and moral compass.
Take heed when the Lord gives you signs and warnings and
wants to get your attention. Do not allow pride and ego to
cause unnecessary drama and hardships, trying to fulfill what the
flesh wants. Obedience is better than sacrifice.

*

We must continually work to actively to understand
our life's journey. In order to move more
efficiently and gain appreciation of self.

*

Sometimes it is better to not know the why. It
is better to just accept and let it flow.

*

We must learn to recognize the actions and character of others
and how they respond and react. Doing so in order to form a
clearer understanding of who you are dealing with and how
to properly respond. Allowing room for the power
to not take offence and move forward.

*

Do not be remiss about doing the right thing.

*

Do not allow yourself to get consumed with potential
negative energy. Allow yourself to be positive in the
present. Control what you can and do not stress off of
what you cannot. Whatever needs to be addressed, do it,
and move past the guilt, regret, or whatever is holding
you back.

*

Just because someone is great, that does not
mean they are great for you. Recognize and
evaluate the character and type of attraction,
deciding if it is truly right for you.

*

In this life, we will come into contact with societies multiple approaches. Do not allow yourself to get sidetracked or out of character when the actions of others do not align with what you deem appropriate and or common sense. Especially if you have already communicated your stance. Do not feed the negative, recognize the reality, and respond accordingly.

*

Never disregard the power and benefits of
having a relationship with YHWH.

*

You do not get to reserve people for later,
simply because you are not ready now.

*

Let love have its perfect place. Do not harbor or feed negativity.

*

Do not intentionally provoke or approach from the hard angles.
Always be mindful of your intention, energy, and focus. What
is your ruling energy? What are you aiming to accomplish
with your actions?

*

The energy that we send out, will be returned. Be
mindful of your presentation and actions.

*

We often think the grass is greener on the other side, but
many times we do not appreciate what we have until its gone. Take
the time to step back and analyze from an objective position and
appreciate where you have been, presently are, and going. Asking
yourself, what is enough?

*

Never minimalize the importance of family.

*

It is never a waste of time going the extra mile to
assure your business is handled properly.

*

Recognize that we all have a trauma membrane. Knowing that
this can and does have a tremendous impact on our outlook and
approach to life and what we deem we need. Realizing that because
of this trauma, healing must occur on a personal internal level or it
will continue to negatively impact all relationships.

*

Do not allow failed expectations to create
resentment or discord in your spirit.

*

If we are too busy caught up in the unknown of
the future or the stress of the past, we rob
ourselves of the opportunity of enjoying the present.

*

Allow room for the natural growth and evolution
of energy and environment and connections
to take place. Pressing is counterproductive and unfair.

*

Differentiate between the platforms we have access to, in
conjunction with our personal desires. You do not have to find
it all in one place. And if what you desire is not present find
the appropriate outlets.

*

Be in the Flow. You never know what
blessings are right around the corner!

*

Being open to experience does not mean that everything
will flow according to plan or expectation. It means that

you are not personally repressing and or holding yourself
back from the opportunity for growth and more. Which
ultimately helps you to invite what is for you into
your life when it is appropriate.

*

Do not be anxious for anything. Trust the process, flow in the
moment, appreciate and be present, and allow life to sort itself
out. Be cognizant of actions and intentions and know that
all things are working together for the good
of those that love YAHWEH.

*

It is always important to be honest and straight forward about
emotions. Even if it might hurt feelings. Say it with love, do
not be callous, but be honest so that no further missteps can
occur, as well as providing an opportunity of choice.

*

Gaining clarity into what makes you tick and like
is never a waste of time. How else will you
discover what is for you if you do not give yourself
the opportunity to be exposed to it.

*

When you Flow with pure intention, there is nothing to worry or stress about. No second guessing, no looking over your shoulders, no remembering lies or stories. Just Flowing and BEing.

*

"Answer not a fool according to his folly, lest thou also be like unto him. Answer a fool according to his folly, lest he be wise in his own conceit."
~Proverbs 26:4-5 King James Version (KJV)

*

"Blessed are they which are persecuted for righteousness' sake: for theirs is the kingdom of heaven."
~ Matthew 5:10 King James Version (KJV)

*

Learn how to be relational without becoming overly attached. A healthy connection, with the ability to separate graciously, if and when needed.

*

Never downplay the power of spontaneity.

*

"Ye are of God, little children, and have overcome them:
because greater is he that is in you, than he that is in the world."
- 1 John 4:4 King James Version (KJV)

*

When dealing with personal apathy or disinterest, infuse a new
approach to your common routine. Find a way to re-engage
and create genuine interest and intrigue. Do not succumb to
the monotony. Adjust perspective to create a new appreciation.

*

Allow honest recognition and reflection to create appreciation
and release tension and negative energy. Controlling what
you can and not stressing off of what you cannot. It is what
it is. The sooner we can come to the realization of it, the
sooner we can process, evaluate, and move accordingly.
Not getting hung up over the same mundane speedbumps
that are not really worth the time or energy we once deemed
necessary. Allow the free flow of love to be. Let a free-flowing
energy exist, and not making waves when not necessary.

*

Appreciate the love that we do receive. Especially when it is
genuine and unconditional. Regardless of the number of people,
embrace who has shown they are for you. Recognizing and

appreciating and embracing your tribe for who they are and what it is. We are all coming from different platforms and perspectives, and as such we all will not see eye to eye. And that is okay. Every puzzle piece does not fit together, but all are needed to make the big picture happen. Embrace your uniqueness.

*

Once the energy of a moment has been experienced,
do not dwell on it. Appreciate it, pull the
lessons from and move forward.

*

'Do not feel bad for outgrowing those who
had the chance to grow with you.'

*

You cannot rush understanding.

*

Be mindful of from whom you are receiving advice
and your guidance from. Consider their
character and track record. Approach everything
with a grain of salt. Taking the meat and
leaving the bones.

*

Be mindful of your intention and energy evoked
and concentrated on. A hearts true earnest
desire will go out and return.

*

Trust what you know. Be open to the Flow, hold
steadfast to your values and foundation,
trust what you see, hear and feel. Do not
yield to the natural, compromising the
supernatural.

*

Remove yourself from taking on the responsibilities of another. We all have a choice and are making decisions. Those decisions create obligations and responsibility. Allow people to fight their own battle and gain the clarity and lessons from them. Be available to help, if truly needed. But, allow people to sort out and process what they create. Do not take on what is not meant for you. Understand your role and boundaries, have clear effective communication, stick to your word, and offer support as needed.

*

Recognize when spiritual, metal, emotional, or
physical test are present. Choose growth and
the idea of "greater than", instead of pleasing the carnal.

*

Do not let impatience cause you to compromise
who you are and everything that you have
worked for. It is not worth it.

*

When a situation or person has revealed its true
character and or energy, trust it. Do not
compromise to be accommodating and or congenial.
Trust what you see, feel, and know.

*

Be mindful to not feed into the negative energy of the world.
Hold steadfast to your faith and hope of a better day. Be very
aware and realistic, while at the same time choosing to see good
and not dwell on what is not. Bring solutions
to the table, not complaints alone.

*

Do the internal work needed to understand
yourself in space and time. Allow yourself to
explore and be exposed to experiences and
things that you are naturally inclined to.

*

Appreciate all that you are presently in space and
time, given all things considered. Do not
allow the day to day to discourage or dissuade
you from your path and dreams.

*

The thing about surprises, you do not know when
they are coming. Trust the process, do not
be anxious for anything.

*

Appreciate and receive the natural comedy of life. Yes, life is
serious, but it is also joyous and jovial as well. Recognize it when
it is present and flow in it, the balance of the serious as well as
the lighthearted.

*

Be secure in what you discern about life. Understand that
you do not know it all. Trust what you have come to learn and
know that it is okay for you to move in a way that protects your
energy while still staying engaged in the process.

*

What are you passionate about?

*

As long as someone or something is not in direct
opposition to you, do not concern yourself
with the negative narratives.

*

When pursuing a life of more, take advantage of
opportunities to rest and relax and recharge.

*

Maintain humility with regards to future perspectives
and opportunities. Remember and keep your moral
compass, always being mindful of your intention, energy,
and focus. Make yourself aware of possibilities both
pro and con. Do not allow the moment to cause your
energy to expand larger than what is true to you.

*

Learn to receive tests as an indication of potential
growth and evolution. Not looking at them as a negative,
but appreciating their presence and for providing
an opportunity to apply what has been earned by
way of experiential understanding and wisdom.

*

It is far better to be present and absorb what is
available in the moment, then to fight for and
press action based off of personal objective.

*

Trust your rules! Do not double back when you
have progressed and moved forward.

*

Speak TRUTH, in love.

*

Whatever we feed, that will grow. Relationships
are no exception. Always be mindful of the rules
of engagement. The energy we exert, our actions,
intentional as well as unintentional, will be mirrored.

*

Do not dwell in offence. Allow room for harmony
and amends to take place. Not allowing
yourself to be naïve, but open and aware at the same time.

*

Pay attention to the energy and actions of those
with ulterior motives. See their actions for

what they are and adjust your behavior and energy
accordingly.

*

Pay attention to your body and its warning signs.
We are spiritual, mental, emotional, and
physical beings. Self-care is important to
continually grow and progress.

*

You never know where your help can come from.

*

Understanding and compromise are needed
to reach a mutual resolution.

*

Patience is a virtue. Obedience is better than sacrifice.

*

You will bear your fruit in your season.

*

Be mindful of the conversations you have and with
whom you have them. Keep relationships

sacred and respectful, being mindful to not cause
any undue drama or negative energy.

*

Life is not guaranteed. Appreciate the moments
that we do have. Express love while we are
able to.

*

Do not move in a way that anticipates the negative.
Be secure and move assuredly, in a way
that has confidence in YHWH paving the way for you.

*

Remain respectful and balanced and appropriate, not
destructive or detrimental while correcting and being a
disciplinarian. None of us are perfect, and we all fall short to
the glory of YHWH. Use constructive criticism and healthy
discipline. Do your best to not leave any situation in negative
energy. Express love and respect to close it out. It is not
about malice and displacement, but correction and growth.

*

Never let anyone or anything knock you off your
square. Starve and disregard distractions.

*

"Blessed is the man that endureth temptation: for
when he is tried, he shall receive the crown of life, which
the Lord hath promised to them that love him."
~ James 1:12 King James Version (KJV)

*

In communication, for maximum reception to take place, it
is not only what is said, but how it is said, as well as when
it is said and by whom it is said. If any of those variables
are off, the likelihood for miscommunication to occur rises
and the message and or intent can be lost in translation.

*

We will never know the full impact of our actions, and the
appreciation that is created and felt, not just from the immediate
benefactor, but others connected to the situation or individual(s)
as well. It is the ripple effect of love and appreciation. Letting love
have its perfect place.

*

Appreciate the LOVE that you wake up to.
Do NOT take any of it for granted.

*

In assessing options, do not be blinded or swayed by the short-term gain. Look at things objectively to see what will yield the greatest return long-term and what will prove to be most beneficial and conducive to the greater mission.

*

If it is meant to be, YAHWEH will provide it.

*

Obstacles only exist if we allow them.

*

Balance and moderation at all times, in all things, in all ways. Understand and appreciate the gift and the responsibility of true power. And with great power, comes great responsibility Which means being mindful and not feeding the excess and catering to the masses. Staying humble, staying grounded, staying focused and rooted on what you are, who you are, and whose you are. "And be not conformed to this world: but be ye transformed by the renewing of your mind, that ye may prove what is that good, and acceptable, and perfect, will of God." Romans 12:2 King James Version (KJV)

*

As a people we need to be more mindful of our energetic disposition and how we approach

and interact with others. People may not always
remember what you say, but they will remember
how you made them feel.

*

At a certain point, we have to let others live their
own lives. Regardless of the relational ties,
everyone is accountable for their own choices and actions.

*

It may not be about what you want, but what you need.

*

Pay attention to the company you keep. Everyone
does not have your best interest at heart,
regardless of length of relationship or relational tie.

*

Meet success with grace and humility.

*

Do not be afraid of the road that lies ahead. The
one that comes with embracing you and
going against the grain.

*

Live a life worth living.

*

Appreciate the time allotted for growth and development.

*

Recognize the bullshit for what it is and keep it
moving. Everyone and every situation are not
worth engaging.

*

Allow blessings to flow through you.

*

Do not let life's' interactions rob you of your grace
and understanding. Remain compassionate
in the face of adversity and trying times.

*

Maintain faith in your patience.

*

It is our job to complete the tasks that YAHWEH
asks of us, while HE facilitates the rest.

Trust the process, and do not give in to
societal, internal, or external pressures.

*

Do not be afraid to speak your raw truth in order
to facilitate growth and healing. If we do not
deal with the real, how can we heal?

*

"Walk the path of your destiny with purpose."

*

Do not allow external attraction to
override internal compatibility.

*

Do not be afraid to let something good go in
favor of getting something greater.

*

As a society we have to be careful what we say
is innate. We must maintain accountability
and responsibility and not scapegoat.

*

How we handle and respond to tests builds our character.

*

Compromise and Peace over Pride and Dissension.

*

Once your position, on a situation you do not
control, has been expressed and properly
communicated, the responsibility is not on you.

*

Do not be stereotypical. Rise above, BE MORE!

*

Be mindful of being judgmental. Make sure you
are doing everything you can to be blameless.

*

"So when they continued asking him, he lifted up
himself, and said unto them, He that is without sin
among you, let him first cast a stone at her."
- John 8:7 King James Version (KJV)

*

"Judge not, that ye be not judged. For with what judgment
ye judge, ye shall be judged: and with what measure
ye mete, it shall be measured to you again. And why
beholdest thou the mote that is in thy brother's eye, but
considerest not the beam that is in thine own eye?"
~ Matthew 7:1-3 King James Version (KJV)

*

Everything that we think, or feel does not need to be expressed
or shared. When we share, we open the opportunity for input
or invitation to accompany, when that may not have been what
was intended.

*

There is nothing wrong with being honest with
yourself about your spiritual, mental, emotional,
or physical state.

*

Embrace your talents and gifts. Do not
cower in the presence of attention.

*

Do not let the fear of losing worldly possessions
cause you to not live your truth.

*

Your rules may not always be the most entertaining,
but they are your rules for a reason.

*

We cannot reject what we ask for when it shows up,
then complain about what we do not have.

*

Wherever you go in the world, people are people. Everything
is a micro of the macro. Recognize and respond accordingly,
being mindful of customs, general societal stereotypes,
character types, and your personal energy.

*

Energy knows no boundaries. It has no limits.

*

If you do not participate in the preparation, you
cannot complain about the execution.

*

Do not wait for someone to fight for your freedom.
Start fighting for your own freedom.

*

Do not entertain what is not for you just for the
sake of being entertained. Be mindful of the
larger picture and potential ramifications.

*

"Every man in his lifetime needs to figure out
what they are running to, from, and why."

*

Sometimes where we are is where we need to be,
regardless of what we might perceive in the
moment.

*

When it is good, appreciate the good. Because it could be bad.

*

Do not let it be about what is "perfect", let
it be about what is right for you.

*

Collect memories.

*

Maximize what is, before you look to "what's next?"

*

If you are living in your past, you are not present in your present.
Pull the lessons from your past to apply them to present
situations, and leave what was, where it is. Work smarter, not
harder, and do not dwell on what was.

*

We cannot complain about what we allow.

*

When engaged in a conversation that has a high potential
to become impassioned, it is important to maintain proper
perspective to ensure efficient effective communication occurs.
This will allow you to deal with the heart and reality of whatever is
being discussed, permitting you to respond, instead of reacting.

*

Appreciate the present. Live in the moment. Embrace the good.

*

Rest when it is time to rest, so that when it is not
time to rest, you will not need to rest.

*

The hard part of doling out tough love, is watching
those that we love process through the
situations their actions caused.

*

Evaluating Relationships

Is it a relationship you are interested in maintaining?
Is the other party making an effort?
Does the relationship add value to your life?
If you are interested, at what point do you remove the
sting of offence(s) from your life? At what point do you
release what was, and embrace what can be? Shit or get
off of the pot, but do not play the fence. It is not fair to
anybody involved, and only delays growth, while potentially
creating new undue tension that must eventually be worked
through. If you choose to stay, Flow and BE, live and let
love, appreciate what is, do not hold on to what was.
How can we expect someone to grow and show us
the "new" behavior if we are too busy holding on to
the mistakes and behavior of the past? We have to
provide the opportunity for growth and change.

*

Never take for granted or doubt that YAHWEH
is always working on the behalf of those
that love and obey HIM, even and especially
when we "cannot see it" or "do not know it".

*

How can you expect to take care of others
if you cannot take care of yourself?

*

Just do it! Just live! Just be! Remove the hesitation, stop
overthinking, and act. You know what is right, and what
is wrong. As long as it is right, and it does not negatively
impact, do it as you can. Remove the what ifs and I wants.
Move strategically and spontaneously through your list.

*

Use what you have available to you to build towards
where you need to be. Do not settle. Be
calculated and mindful of what is available and continue to grow.

*

Appreciate the blessing of being able to be a blessing.

*

Be mindful of the energy in your presentation.

*

Today's vision is not always for an immediate
moment. It can be a preview of where we are
headed as long as we take care of what
is for us to take care of today.

*

Take advantage of opportunities to build
relationship. When common ground is present,
invest in the energy of the moment.

*

48 Laws of Power: Rule No. 1:
Never outshine the master;
"Always make those above you feel
comfortably superior and brilliant."

*

Do not be accommodating to the point that it is
detrimental. You cannot pour from an empty
cup. And the branch that bends too much eventually breaks.

*

<u>We are a composite of signs, not simply the final result.</u>

The month and day and time that we are born is all significant and represents the culmination of a transformative process. When we are born, depending on our numbers, we are assigned a sign. For myself, I was born September 30th. This qualifies me as a Libra. However, as I am growing in my understanding, one of the revelations that came to me, was that I am not simply just a Libra. A libra in the sense that based on my numbers that is the sign that is attributed, however my gestation period lasted much longer than the window of Libra. The totality of my gestation was three distinct and transformative trimesters. During each stage, I was exposed to multiple lunar and solar shifts, experiencing various seasons, being developed through a set of signs that were needed in order to make me. My ingredients. Qualities & all.

For Example.

<u>Conception:</u>

1st month) Aquarius: Jan 21- Feb 18, The Water Bearer, The 11th Sign

2nd month) Pisces: Feb 19 – March 20, Two Fishes, The 12th Sign.

3rd month) Aries: March 21- April 20, The Ram, The 1st Sign.

4th month) Taurus: April 21- May 21, The Bull, The 2nd Sign.

5th month) Gemini: May 22- June 21, The Heavenly Twins, The 3rd Sign.

6th month) Cancer: June 22-July 22, The Crab, The 4th Sign.

7th month) Leo: July 23- Aug 23, The Lion and King of the Beast, The 5th Sign.

8th month) Virgo: Aug 24-Sep 22, The Virgin, The 6th Sign.

<u>Birth:</u> 9th month) Libra: Sept 23 – Oct 23, The Scales, The 7th Sign.

*

And be not conformed to this world: but be ye transformed by the renewing of your mind, that ye may prove what is that good, and acceptable, and perfect, will of God.
~ Romans 12:2 King James Version (KJV)

*

Gratitude & Acceptance.

*

If you do not want it to be about you, do not make it about you.

*

"Greater love hath no man than this, that a man lay down his life for his friends." ~ John 15:13 King James Version (KJV)

*

It is not always about what we want, but what is needed, which can prove to be vastly more valuable.

*

Ethics over emotions.

*

Figure out what feeds your happy.

*

On this grand journey of life, we will encounter and embark on many other voyages along the way. All serving a purpose to help us get to our final destination. Be open to experiences and what can be learned and gained from them. Everything happens for a reason, and it either last for a season or for a lifetime. We do not always know in the moment, so be open to endings and beginnings. Accepting them for the steps that they are.

*

"A fair exchange is not a robbery."

*

Appreciate and embrace simplicity and
ease when they are present.

*

Never settle just because it is something
that you may have wanted.

*

Maintaining emotional control is essential
to preserving focus on priorities.

*

Never feel ashamed for being proud of yourself
for completing goals and accomplishments,
regardless of the size. It is more than okay
and encouraged. We have to be
our biggest supporters.

*

Just as nature goes through seasons, so do our lives. As we go
through these seasons, until we gain understanding of the process,
it can feel overwhelming as our lives are constantly going through
something. It is important to realize that you are not crazy, yes, we
are always going through something and we are constantly growing

and evolving and experiencing. With this understanding, we can then begin to objectively look at what is taking place, analyzing why it is taking place, and recognizing patterns of what is taking place when it is taking place. This ability to recognize self in present space and time, recognizing which season of your life you are in, can help illuminate what is specifically needed from or being presented to you. Helping you to move with more confidence and clarity and perspective. Easing tension and stressors. Making this journey a little more manageable.

*

When moments of clarity have been presented, as much as possible, take advantage of the opportunity to sit in the lesson(s) and let them take root. Absorb the energy and the intention of the lesson, allowing it to make the necessary adjustments to character and behavior.

*

Words speak to who we esteem to be.
Actions speak to who we truly are.

*

Everything is being provided.

*

It is not about how it will be received. It is about being the vessel and not allowing our ego and sense of self to stand in the way of what has been divinely imparted in to and asked of us. Our job is to be the vessel. It is YAHWEHS job to decide how it will be received.

*

In as many ways as possible, nurture growth. Do not appease complacency or the comfort zones of our life.

*

It is essential that we identify and embrace those unique truths and inclinations that make us who we are.

*

Though it is good to give and share, everything that we have available to us, is not meant for everyone else. Let what is for you, be for you.

*

Remove the expectation and necessity of immediate perfection and move towards a space of enjoying the journey of working towards it.

*

Wherever you go, there you are. The grass is not
always greener on the other side of town. It
is greener where you water it.

*

"You cannot go to freedom school on scholarship from pharaoh."
– Jesse Jackson

*

As we go along this journey of ascension, it is
important to not lose you. No matter what
transpires, stay true to your principals, and
values, and morals. Your foundation.
When a plants roots reach the edge of the pot, it needs to
be transplanted. Maximize your life where you presently
are, and if a transplanting needs to take place in order to
continue your journey, do not be afraid to make that step.
Gain some fresh perspective, increase your growth
potential, surround yourself with fertile opportunities.

*

Calculated risks.

*

It does not serve our higher self to feed into lower
energy. Continue to recognize when a test
is being presented and do what is necessary to rise above.

*

We cannot allow ourselves to become more energetic about
someone else's dream than they are. Or more than we are about
our own dreams and aspirations. It is okay to support, but we
must make ourselves a priority.

*

It does no good to wallow in the lack.

*

As we gain knowledge of self in space and time, it is important
to distinguish the various relationship types and those in our
life that occupy those spaces. It is important to respect and
understand the platform of each relationship, and not inflect
characteristics from a different relationship type onto one
another. And if a relational interaction is desired that is not
present, it is incumbent upon us to do the work to cultivate it.

*

It is not about getting it done the quickest,
it is about getting it done right.

*

As we grow in understanding of self in space in time, we
inevitably begin to recognize and sort out what is and what
is not for us. As we go through this filtration process, it
is important to not be over analytical in the process, and
allow room for nuance and the unaccounted for, as
well as error. For none of us are perfect, and we all fall short.

*

Never let anyone else define you.

*

Never let the journey of ascension be about
revenge. Keep the energy and intention pure.

*

Do not forget to laugh!

*

If you believe you are trapped, you will be. If
you believe you are free, you will be.

*

The only way to satiate that hunger and
void, is by walking boldly in purpose.

That will provide the only true fulfillment.

*

Streamline and consolidate. Cluttered space, cluttered life.

*

"It does not do us well to dwell on dreams and forget to live."
– Dumbledore

*

"It is not our abilities that show what we
truly are, it is our choices."
– Dumbledore

*

Harness your power presence.

*

Do not let your food get cold staring at someone else's plate.

*

"Soon we must all face the choice between
what is right, and what is easy."
-Dumbledore

*

You do not need permission to do what
you know you already need to do.

*

Do not wait for death to bring you to life.

*

You can only live one life, and that is your life.
You cannot be bogged down with how
others choose to live theirs.

*

Do not be pressed to interact with those who are not engaging
and reciprocating in the process, regardless of their affluence or
position. And in the same breath, appreciate and engage those
that are showing up, making an effort, and willing to reciprocate.

*

Identify your weaknesses and make them strengths.
Do not give anyone or anything the
opportunity to use them against you.

*

6) "Be careful for nothing; but in every thing by
prayer and supplication with thanksgiving let your

requests be made known unto God. And the peace
of God, which passeth all understanding, shall keep
your hearts and minds through Christ Jesus."
- Philippians 4:6-7 King James Version (KJV)

*

"For as the body without the spirit is dead,
so faith without works is dead also."
- James 2:14-26 King James Version (KJV)

*

Do not go backwards out of frustration.

*

You cannot play in the mud and not get dirty.

*

Intention. Energy. Focus.

*

If it does not just involve you, it is not
just about you. It is about us.
Meet people where they are at, compromise
and be understanding.
Identify and fulfill your role.

*

On this journey of ascension, getting your foot in the door and
establishing a connection is not always about the appearance
of the initial opportunity presented. That opportunity might
not be "ideal", but it will provide the needed introduction, and
if properly executed can lead to unexpected blessings.

*

Once a cognitive stretch has occurred, the
knowledge of more will always be present.

*

Pressure is applied to check the integrity.

*

Distinguish between what has true value and
what has had "value" placed on it.

*

Your voice matters. You deserve to be heard. Do not be afraid
to voice your truths. Do not accommodate solely out of the fear of
creating a tense or competitive moment. Speaking your truth allows
you to be heard and have input on what will transpire as well as possibly
offer the audience a perspective they may not have considered.

*

Be assertive in action.

*

Cut out destructive qualities and actions early.
Do not let it take root and develop into
counterproductive behavior later.

*

Morals, are never for sale or negotiable.

*

Make sure you know what is asked and expected of you.

*

Do not give the enemy an ounce of help. Work to
be blameless. It is not about how fast or the
flashiest most exciting, it is about doing it right.
One step, one day, one moment at a time.
Slow and steady wins the race.

*

Understand and respect the value of your time.

*

Do not put all of your eggs in one basket.

Build a network of like minds to collaborate
and build and source from.

*

Establish boundaries. Spiritually.
Mentally. Emotionally. Physically.
Understanding where you are going is far more
important than how fast you get there.

*

When YAHWEH blocks it, leave it alone!

*

People reveal themselves through their actions. Pay attention.

*

When you take what reveals itself at face value,
you will be armed with all you need,
to spot what your next move must be when encountered again.

*

Life is precious. Appreciate it and the people that you do have.

*

"The flower that blooms in adversity is the
most beautiful and rare of them all."
-Mulan

*

When you are legitimately done with something,
do not let someone else talk you back into
re-engaging it.

*

Do not feel pressured to execute your entire plan in one day.
Do not over-extend yourself. Execute methodically.
Efficiently and effectively without pressing
or spreading yourself too thin.

*

Knowing that a situation or relationship is not built for the long
haul is not necessarily a negative. Knowing this gives you the
foresight to plan ahead and have an idea as to how things
may unfold. Take advantage of this knowledge.

*

You cannot save someone from them self. We all
have to be accountable for our choices.

*

Evolution is not a one-way street. Continued
poor choices and actions create and foster
regression.

*

With business, its business. Get the
emotion and relation out of it.

*

Understand the matrix and the opposition. Formulate
a plan and beat them at their own game.

*

Do not rob us of your full potential.

*

Sometimes it is better that we do not receive what we ask for.
What is waiting for us could be exactly
what we need and vastly better.

*

Do not be moved by the ignorance of others.
Let them bask in their own stupidity.

*

You do not know what you do not know.

*

"It's not who you are underneath, it's
what you do that defines you."
-Rachel, Batman Begins

*

Understand the responsibilities associated with
your purpose, so that you know what is
expected of you and how to invest your time and
energy effectively and efficiently, allowing
you to move methodically.

*

Be wholly authentic.

*

Know, appreciate, and embrace your worth.

*

Never help begrudgingly.

*

"Money does not get you to where you need to
go, you get you to where you need to go"
~ Dame Dash

*

Keep your message consistent. Evolving, but consistent.

*

Learn to monetize what you love.

*

"Don't be the leaf that flows with the river,
be the stone that splits the stream."
-Sorry To Bother You

*

Loose lips sink ships.

*

Be responsible about what you are responsible for.

*

A leader has to see the big picture as well as the immediate.
They are not allowed the luxury of staying
surface level in processing and action.

*

If you are playing the power game, power
only acquiesce to power.

*

People do not mind helping people who
are willing to help themselves.

*

There is always someone watching.

*

Do not forget to take personal time to recharge and re-center.

*

Delivering straight forward no frill concise
communication can yield immediate clarity and
results.

*

When receiving help from others, sometimes
they do not recognize the urgency of the
situation, the pace that we are moving at,
and what we are needing from them.

When this occurs, the responsibility is ours to
convey this so that we can move efficiently and
effectively.

*

There will be times where we will have to take a
hard stance against and do things towards
people we love and care about in order to
establish boundaries and understanding.

*

Celebrate life and community. Appreciate
the moments within the moments.

*

Be intentional with your time, energy, and finances.
Take accountability and responsibility for
how they are used. Develop a healthy pace,
allowing you to continually build and progress
without burning out.

*

Exposure. Trial and Error. Maturation. Reincarnation.

*

There are people that care about you more than you realize.

*

Do not force relationships. Allow people to do
what they want to do so that you can see what
they would rather do.

*

Do not make the mistake of thinking that everyone
is flowing by the same moral code.

*

You will not always know what your opposition looks like.
Do not be fooled by first impressions.

*

Take advantage of your talents and gifts. Learn
how to leverage your power presence.

*

Survey the societal landscape, see what is being
provided, see what is lacking, see where you
fit in and what you can bring to the table.

*

People have to want better for themselves, and until
they do, as long as you feed their energy
you make yourself susceptible to the
consequences and repercussions.

*

Accept realities for what they are.
Believe what is being presented.

*

Sometimes the voice of reason needed
comes from the unlikeliest of sources.

*

You can ruin a good thing by moving too fast.

*

Be like a duck letting water roll off its back.
Allow trials and tribulations to flow off easily.
Flow and BE!

*

Never give someone so much power over your life
that if they make a decision against you
your flow stops.

*

Do not succumb to energetic castration.
Harness your power presence.

*

"It's all good when we are viewed as an ally for their
cause, the tip of their spear for their issues.
Once the tables turn and we are in a position of
power over them, their energy changes to
one that feels threatened. They feel we are being
condescending and demeaning to them.
That we are now, too intense."

*

Appreciation without settling.

*

Do not allow societal realities to dictate your creative output.

*

Do not make stupid decisions a habit.

*

"Never did they tell you to give up on the child that you were..."
~ Xavier Gipson

*

Harness the pure energy that existed within you before the
contamination of life's circumstances intervened.

*

Occurrences that may initially appear as a setback
could actually be a blessing in disguise.

*

Obedience is better than sacrifice. We do not
know the ripple effect of a bad decision.

*

Evolve and change or stay the same and repeat.

*

Exposing yourself to new environments and
interactions builds the potential energy needed
for your kinetic release in new opportunities.

*

It is always about principles and character.
It is not about what is the easiest or quickest
or allows you to scapegoat the issue.

*

Provide disciplinary action with a measure of grace in the early
stages, before poor choices become bad habits. Doing so in
an effort to avoid having someone operating outside of the
realm of grace dole out disciplinary actions
that could yield far greater damage.

*

Harness you power presence. Fortify your defense.
Each new level brings with it a set of new
threats and weapons meant to destroy you.
Stay true in who you are, what you are,
and what you represent. Do not be swayed.
Stay strong in your principles and morals.
Maintain all love always. Always be mindful.
Always be aware. Always the greater.
Never the lesser.

*

Do not disrespect your blessings.

*

We are not responsible for the presumptions of others.

*

Recognize and understand your triggers
and how to properly address them.

*

There are opportunities that exist that we are not even aware of.

*

Good or bad, we do not know what we do not know. We
must learn to stand firm in what we do know, while being
open to realizing that as we grow through what we go
through, there will be new blessings, lessons, opportunities,
and allies as well as trials, pitfalls, and opposition.

*

Find the balance between being inspired and motivated
to continually grow and progress while not getting caught
up in the "keeping up with the jones" external imagery
that is presented. Be at peace with growing at your own
pace, blossoming in your own season, when it your turn.

*

The grace period for excuses has expired!

*

When I was a child,

I speak as a child,

I understood as a child,

I thought as a child:

but when I became a man, I put away childish things.

~ 1 Corinthians 13:11 King James Version (KJV)

*

You cannot be great without facing and conquering your fears.

*

There are times when we will have to do what hurts

in order to heal, grow, and more forward.

*

Hard, sharp, refined, and streamlined. Not

cold, demeaning, apathetic, or callous.

More defense and fortitude than abrasive and antagonizing.

*

"A wise man surrounds himself with likeminded

people to help fulfill and carry out the mission,

empowering them in the process."

*

If it does not involve you, it does not need to involve you.

*

"Consistency is harder when no one is clapping
for you. You must clap for yourself during
those times. You should always be your biggest fan."

*

"I love the lotus because while growing from mud, it is unstained."
-Zhou Dunyi

*

Lotus Energy: Creation and cosmic
renewal and "Primordial Purity."

*

"Sometimes Yahweh allows our feelings to be
hurt, to ensure that our purpose is birthed,
that we understood our worth and we get back to work."
- Rae Holliday

*

We can make this journey as easy or as difficult as we want.
When we know what we know and have our direction, we
can act immediately with purpose, urgency, and faith or

we can delay, going through additional trial and error, only
to arrive back at the place we started realizing that the
understanding and direction we received was correct.

*

More work is more work, however this means
the greater the reward as well.

*

Vulnerability is relatable.

*

Maintain gratitude in the face of adversity.

*

Sometimes people want to see more
from you before they invest.

*

Direct your energy appropriately for those it is meant for.

*

"The thief cometh not, but for to steal, and to kill,
and to destroy: I am come that they might have life,
and that they might have it more abundantly."
- John 10:10 King James Version (KJV)

*

We may not be for everybody, but we are for somebody. Allow whatever is within to flow out and be received by whomever it is meant for. Give yourself an opportunity to find your tribe.

*

Allow petty situations to remove petty people from your life.

*

Realities are not always pleasant, but it is reality.

*

Extremes reveal truths.

*

We cannot force anyone to be more than they presently are. That is something that everyone must decide for themselves.

*

The family that we start out with is not always the family we end up with.

*

Do not stress off of the unknown. Cross that bridge if and when you approach it.

*

What becomes is not always what was intended.

*

In order for the continued growth and evolution of
a relationship to occur, all parties involved
must be willing to swallow their pride and
do whatever is necessary to
compromise, contribute, heal, and resolve.

*

Being at the helm is not about comfort zones.
It is about stepping into that leadership
position and embracing and tackling the
responsibilities regardless of want or ease.

*

Start with YAHWEH. Stay with
YAHWEH. End with YAHWEH.

*

"Hard work beats talent when talent does not work hard."

*

Allow being disheartened to fortify, not cripple.

*

There comes a time when the prince becomes the king.

*

"They soon forgat his works; they waited not for his counsel."
-Psalm 106:13 King James Version (KJV)

*

Do not be a prisoner of the moment and completely dismiss and
or forget all of the lessons learned from the similar times you
have had and the storms you have weathered and overcame.

*

"Go where you are celebrated not where you are tolerated."

*

Momentum does not build itself.

*

Hand crafting your life means that you accept the uncertainty
of not being able to rely on programmed comfort zones.
However, it also inherently possesses the freedom of expression
and excitement of uncertainty because you realize that there
are no ceilings. The only thing that truly limits you, is you.

*

The birthing process is not pleasant, it does
not" feel good", but it is necessary.

*

Balance and moderation in all things at all times in all things.

*

As you grow, it is not always you that changes or
begins to act differently, many times it is
those around you that adjust their behavior towards you.

*

Life is a marathon. It is important to start and finish strong. This
is a journey of endurance. Do not spread yourself too thin by
putting more on your plate than you can eat. You can always
add to, but once it is present, it will require
more effort to balance it all out.
Move methodically and balanced.

*

Do not count your chickens before they hatch.

*

Do not give away wins. Do all that is needed
to ensure you receive all that is for you.

*

Be honest with yourself and where your heart is.

*

Do not give someone multiple chances to disappoint you.
Once you recognize behavior, trust it and adjust accordingly.

*

"Now faith is the substance of things hoped
for, the evidence of things not seen."
- Hebrews 11:1 King James Version (KJV)

*

Do not keep pressing towards anything that
YAHWEH is keeping you away from.

*

Do not take unnecessary risks.

*

"You cannot fit in where you stand out."
-Ja Rule

*

The buffers and façade will only get you so far.
At some point authenticity must be.

*

Do not let emotions or relational ties get
in the way of prudent business.
Do not compromise your position to strengthen another's.

*

"Trust in the LORD with all thine heart; and lean
not unto thine own understanding. In all thy ways
acknowledge him, and he shall direct thy paths."
- Proverbs 3:5-6 King James Version (KJV)

*

Do not allow yourself to become paralyzed by emotion.
Give yourself the space to process what you are
feeling without letting it paralyze your actions.

*

"Sometimes when we feel we have been buried
we have actually been planted. Bloom."

*

A no in one instance can be a yes in another.
Do not adopt a spirit of defeat.

*

When people are used to you being the strong one holding
everything together, they frequently do not recognize or
understand that you are capable of hurting or how you are
hurting. Do not be afraid to communicate
how you feel and that you need help.

*

"Do not put the hustle before the art."
~ Tracy Morgan

*

Adjust your energy and temperament according
to your environment and parties involved. A
sharp demeanor needed with some, may not and
probably is not the best course of action with
all. This approach has the potential to
negatively impact and or offend.

*

Find a way to accomplish opportunities that you
may feel you are not qualified for. Do not just say
no, figure out a way to communicate your needs
and abilities in order to fulfill the request.

*

Operating from a place of faith means controlling what we can
and getting out of the way. We cannot say that we are trusting
YAHWEH to provide then take it upon ourselves to move
in a way that undermines and interjects our will
and understanding into the equation.
If we say we trust, then we need to trust.

*

Sometimes a problem has more than one element
needed to bring about its complete resolution. Do not
be discouraged when one element is completed, and the
overall problem has not been resolved. Appreciate knowing
that you are being proactive, and that it is not a matter
of if, but when. Sometimes something is better than nothing.

*

While going through your own personal transitions
and obstacles, do not be insensitive to the

fact that others are going through transitions
and obstacles of their own.
Have compassion in the face of adversity.

*

Let recognition come naturally and organically.
Do not be vain in seeking out manufactured admiration.

*

Let your actions authenticate your words.

*

YOUR plan is not for everybody and will not be
understood by everybody. And that is okay.
If you possess the conviction, you must maintain
your faith and stick to the script.
Even and especially in the face of doubters and detractors.

*

Do not set yourself up for disappointment by
creating expectations for things that you do not
have any control over. Control what you can
and do not stress off of the rest.
Being mindful to not make or take anything personal.

*

Be careful of the lure of monetary advancement.
It is not about acquiring at ANY cost.
Keep morals and goals in perspective and in check.

*

Allow your gifts to be a blessing to others.

*

Do not be greedy!
Appreciate and eat what is on your plate, not
comparing to what is on another's.

*

The blessings that we put out will come back to
us. Be open to receiving. Do not let negative
emotion fester and cause you to spite your blessings.

*

There will be times when we will have to remind others
who we are. Life's situations and circumstances can
create discord and breakdown. When this occurs, we are
presented with an opportunity. We must meet the discord
head on in order to bring about clarity and reestablish
our energetic presence, while building rapport and respect.

*

Vulnerability and openness strengthen relationships.
People want to feel included and valued,
as well as engaged and appreciated.

*

Everything has a breaking point.

*

A useful tool on one level can prove to be a detriment
on the next. Do not hold on to what is
no longer beneficial, release it in order to
allow room to embrace new tools.

*

Everything that is taking place around us
is not a direct reflection of us.
Do not take everything so personally.

*

Appreciate moments of isolation to restore energy
and gain clarity of perspective and journey. Having
things removed can initially seem like a setback
or punishment, however it could be you
are having distractions removed to simplify
and have your line of sight improved.

*

You will have to fight to acquire and maintain your position.

*

Embrace and recognize opportunities that
can come as a result of a door closing.
What is being taken away with the left is
being provided for with the right.

*

You train your whole life for your moment.
All of those other times that you thought
you were ready, you weren't.
If it was time, it would have happened.

*

As we authentically move towards our destiny,
beneficial energies and people will be
made available to and for us.

*

You are more than enough and possess what it takes to succeed.

*

Give your ideas the respect of treating
them like a tangible attainable goal.

*

Do not ignore the signs that you asked
YAHWEH to show you.

*

Never compromise your foundation and
what has been established.

*

Learn to help without inflicting harm to self.

*

Never compromise your power presence.
Compromise your approach or actions to
meet a solution, but never compromise
your respect or power presence.

*

Give people the respect and chance to respond to your
honesty. Do not lead on or paint a false narrative. Keep it
real. Allow them to choose whether or not they would like to
continue. They might surprise you and say yes and provide
you what you need out of respect and appreciation.

*

A new approach yields new results.
Do not be dismayed when the view is not
the same as you are used to.
Embrace the new, embrace the change.

*

Do not bring old energy to your new environment.
Allow what was to remain, where it is at.
Embrace all that your new environment has to offer.
Do not allow yourself to be robbed of what awaits you.

*

Sometimes you have to fly one plane
while you build another one.

*

Make the time to feed those neglected areas of your life.

*

You cannot do business with everybody. And that
is okay. Understand and accept this and
build with those that are like minded.

*

Your business partners do not have to be your
friends. If it mixes, beautiful, if not, do not force
it. Do not be afraid to venture out and do business
with "strangers" and build relationships.

*

Whenever the feeling of being off track occurs, get back to
the basics. Remember and implement the fundamentals. Those
things that laid the foundation to get you where you are
today.

*

"He that refuseth instruction despiseth his own soul:
but he that heareth reproof getteth understanding."
– Proverbs 15:32 King James Version (KJV)

*

Be proactive and remove the opportunity for
others to point out to you what you already
know you need to accomplish, especially when
it is something that impacts others.

*

Recognize and embrace truths as soon as they
are presented and respond accordingly.

*

Be supportive and sympathetic without adding personal issues.

*

If you will not go after what you want, you
cannot complain about what shows up.

*

Be a wolf, go get it.

*

"Sometimes it is better to stay a bit hungry until
the odds improve rather than expend precious
energy on a fruitless chase."
– livingwithwolves.com

*

"Perfection is never an accident. To achieve something great,
it takes the vision to see your goal and the hard work to get
there. The views from the mountain top are made that more
beautiful by the struggle it took to climb the peak."
– Rev Run

*

Being honest with others about your
emotions is not disrespectful.
It is not what is felt, but how it is expressed.

*

Knowing who you do not want to be can help
shape who you do want to become.

*

Results come about from attainable goals.

*

Elevation is not always a vertical process.

*

You cannot force someone to accept your help.

*

"There is a way which seemeth right unto a man,
but the end thereof are the ways of death."
- Proverbs 14:12 King James Version (KJV)

*

Sometimes it is advantageous to initially
intentionally place yourself in a compromised

position in order to neutralize the

situation and later gain leverage.

*

With so much taking place around us, we must be

mindful to not allow anything or anyone to

knock us off of our square. We must remain

prudent. We must not only withstand the

onslaught, but we must also rise to the

occasion and overcome all obstacles.

We must turn walls into speedbumps.

Constantly owning our power presence.

Obeying principles and morals, using wisdom,

and respecting the signs that we asked for.

Staying the course and appreciating what has been established.

*

Much of what we see today that is established and self-propelling took years to establish. How many more years are you going to allow your imagination manifestation to be delayed? Do not be daunted by the proposition of your dreams taking years to establish. The time will pass anyways. The longer you take to start, the longer it will take to materialize.

*

16) "Behold, I send you forth as sheep in the midst of wolves: be ye therefore wise as serpents, and harmless as doves. But beware of men: for they will deliver you up to the councils, and they will scourge you in their synagogues; And ye shall be brought before governors and kings for my sake, for a testimony against them and the Gentiles. But when they deliver you up, take no thought how or what ye shall speak: for it shall be given you in that same hour what ye shall speak. For it is not ye that speak, but the Spirit of your Father which speaketh in you."
~ Matthew 10:16-20 King James Version (KJV)

*

Unless you are planning on living off of the grid, we will come in to contact with the full spectrum of personality and character types. Understand that if a product or service is being offered, if you are not aiming for a direct niche audience, everything that you say and or do is attached to what you represent and offer. If you are aiming for maximum exposure find a way to separate personal from professional. Have your professional operate as a separate entity with its own characteristics and personality while you maintain your personal. This will allow you to not be backed into a corner or unintentionally isolate or alienate.

Speak truth to conflict to bring about resolution
and allow clear informed decisions to take place.

The truth has one story. Not yours, mines and
the truth. Be honest and vulnerable.
That is the only way to fully move through it all.

*

Let your actions be your equity.

*

Clarity, when brought about through painful and
or stressful situations, is always a blessing.

*

"No weapon formed against me shall prosper. This is not
saying no weapons shall be formed. They will. This is not
saying no weapons will be used. They will. Its saying build all
you want. Try all you want. But no weapon formed against
me shall prosper. For I am more than a conqueror. I have
been tried and tried before. And I have been victorious.
For I recognize that I am not fighting this battle alone and
greater is HE that is within me than he that is within the
world. I recognize this. And I choose to rise above."

*

Morals and values are the real treasures. Never downplay that.

*

As we navigate through this life it is important for us
to take time to reflect and process self in space and
time. Gain understanding of our energetic frequency
in conjunction with your surroundings. Recognize what
truly feeds and nourishes. What is the best method of
delivery for your talents and gifts? Not what is the popular
answer or what is expected. But what is true to us.

*

Continue to operate with a sense of justice and morals, allowing
the poison that others spew to ruin them while you stand in
your truth continuing to flourish and rise above. Allow your
actions to be your social currency. Interact with those that
see the truth and do not be swayed by those that do not.
Never force anyone to be on your side or interact with you.

*

Appreciate the evolution of you.

*

Never scoff at any amount of growth. Especially if
you feel it is "insignificant" or "little". Overtime those
"little" "insignificant" growths all add up. They all
help to build and establish and sustain all that you
are, becoming, and will encounter. It all adds up.

*

It is not just about getting the work done, it is about

harnessing your power presence as you

accomplish tasks and move forward. It is okay, be a wolf.

*

Understand the level of your calling and what

is needed and called of and for you.

*

"You must be shapeless, formless, like water. When you

pour water in a cup, it becomes the cup. When you pour

water in a bottle, it becomes the bottle. When you pour

water in a teapot, it becomes the teapot. Water can

drip and it can crash. Become like water my friend."

-Bruce Lee

*

36) "For what shall it profit a man, if he shall gain the whole

world, and lose his own soul? Or what shall a man give in

exchange for his soul? Whosoever therefore shall be ashamed

of me and of my words in this adulterous and sinful generation;

of him also shall the Son of man be ashamed, when he

cometh in the glory of his Father with the holy angels."

- Mark 8:36-38 King James Version (KJV)

*

Everyone's action is not of pure intention. Be
mindful of wolves in sheep's clothing.

*

"Don't be in a hurry to condemn because he doesn't
do what you do or think as you think or
as fast. There was a time when you didn't
know what you know today."
-Malcolm X

*

Falling apart to come together. During transition and
transformation, it can feel as if everything is falling apart.
In reality everything is coming together and aligning for
your highest good. You are being pushed to evolve and
get out of your comfort zones so that you can live
and experience your true greatness. Welcome change.

*

Stay true to you. Never lose or compromise your
authenticity no matter what heights you
scale.

*

Do not keep investing into a mistake just because
you have already invested time and money
on it. Restart as many times a s you need.

*

Conception to Consumption.

*

Do not feel as if you have to be constrained to
one career or one lane. Live your life as your
energy is flowing. Enjoy and embrace the seasons.

*

"For God hath not given us the spirit of fear; but
of power, and of love, and of a sound mind."
~ 2 Timothy 1:7 King James Version (KJV)

*

Loyalty is not an external process. It should have nothing
to do with outside tangible circumstantial factors. Which
is why it should not be placed blindly. If loyalty is tied to
circumstances or people, instead of internal fortitude, it
is subject to change as circumstances change. Be mindful
what you pledge your loyalty too and whose pledging loyalty
to you or a circumstance that you have orchestrated.

*

Know your limits.

*

Do not be so thirsty for opportunity that you
drink from any cup, that is how you get
poisoned.

*

Always for a Reason, either for a Season or a Lifetime.
Learn to embrace seasonal relationships and experiences.
Everything and everyone is not meant for the totality of our
lifetime and that is okay. Appreciate the moments, experiences,
lessons, and tools gained from these seasonal exchanges.

*

Do not allow your potential energy to become toxic.
Release and use it appropriately, allowing room for new energy.

*

Do not interrupt your opposition when
they are making a mistake.

*

Sometimes we have not failed enough.

*

"F.E.A.R: Fail Early And Responsibly"
-Robert Kiyosaki

*

Appreciate the ability to look back on pain and trials and laugh.

*

Tough decisions strengthen our resolve and
mental fortitude. Allowing us to gain greater
control over our emotional response and influence.

*

Hesitation when action is required can be
costly. Be swift when clarity is achieved.

*

Recognize and appreciate those who support
you without you even having to ask.

*

YAHWEH will put you back together right
in front of the people that broke you.

*

Do not allow money or monetary gain to make you
move. Do not make it a M.O.M. and P.O.P
operation, Money Over Morals and Profits Over Principles.

*

Be open to the non-conventional and what
you may have deemed to be not for you.

*

Committing the same mistakes over and over shows
a lack of preparedness for the next level.
Do not allow bad mistakes to become bad behavior.

*

As much as things change and evolve, there are
some things that always stay the same.

*

Build your future today. That tree that has been
around for generations, was not planted
yesterday. Start your generational abundance today.

*

Do not build up this life to be more complicated
than it really is. Not the relationships, but life.

Life by itself, is not difficult. We must get
back in touch with the simplicity.

*

"Who I was, is not who I have to be. I have the freedom
and right to evolve and change. I do not have to
stay the same, like the same things, or want the same
things. In fact, it is beneficial for me to accept and
embrace change. Change is where I am headed."

*

Do not entertain tests. Recognize the triggers for what they
are and do not indulge or invest any time and energy into them.
Know that they are not beneficial for you. The slightest
inappropriate engagement is too costly.
That juice is not worth the squeeze.

*

YAHWEH did not send Moses to negotiate with Pharaoh.

*

Start the wave, do not ride it.

*

No matter what we do, we cannot rush our season. Trying to
do so can be detrimental and costly by having us miss out on
what is present while we are preoccupied with what is not meant
for us at that moment.

*

Never argue with a fool.

*

Helping another on their path can help illuminate our own.

*

Do not let that big caring heart of yours get you in trouble.

*

Do not be what they expect you to be. Be more.

*

"Before you heal someone, ask him if he is willing
to give up the things that made him sick."
-Hippocrates

*

"The world needs my energy."

*

Some journeys we have to walk alone.

*

Do not fear asking for what is yours.

*

We cannot allow the bad habits of another to inhibit us.

*

Do not get involved doing business with people
who are not serious about doing business.

*

"The Bible Story of Joseph, from the Book of Genesis,
is one of heroic redemption and forgiveness. Joseph was the
most loved son of his father, Israel, given the famous robe of many
colors. When Joseph reported having dreams of his brothers,
and even the stars and moon, bowing before him, their jealousy of
Joseph grew into action. The brothers sold him into slavery to a
traveling caravan of Ishmaelites who took him to Egypt and sold
him to Potiphar, the captain of Pharaoh's guard.

In Egypt, the Lord's presence with Joseph enables him to find favor with Potiphar and the keeper of the prison. With God's help, Joseph interprets the dreams of two prisoners, predicting that one of them will be reinstated but the other put to death. Joseph then interprets the dreams of the Pharaoh, which anticipate seven years of plenty followed by seven years of famine. Pharaoh recognizes Joseph's God-given ability and prompts his promotion to the chief administrator of Egypt.

Shortage of food in Canaan forces Jacob to send his sons to buy grains from the Egyptians. Benjamin, Joseph's younger brother remains at home as Jacob fears of losing him, as he did Joseph. When Joseph finally encounters his brothers again, he deliberately conceals his identity. He accuses them of being spies and tells them to return with Benjamin or he will not sell them grain. The ongoing famine forces Jacob to reluctantly send his sons back to Egypt with Benjamin, and they are unexpectedly invited to dine at Joseph's house.

Joseph then tests the character of his brothers by placing a silver cup the sack of Benjamin and falsely accusing him of theft. When Judah offers to stay in place of Benjamin, Joseph knows that his character has changed and reveals that he is their brother. Joseph explains they need not feel guilty for betraying him as it was God's plan for him to be in Egypt to preserve his family. He told them to bring their father and his entire household into Egypt to live in the province of Goshen because there were five more years of famine left. Joseph supplied them Egyptian transport wagons, new garments, silver, and twenty additional donkeys carrying provisions for the journey. Jacob is then joyously reunited with his son Joseph."

-www.biblestudytools.com

*

Do not allow the negative moments to completely erase and drown out the positive moments. Appreciate the good for the good.

*

Whatever we are pursuing, is pursuing us as well.

*

Acquire assets not liabilities.

*

Vanity is not your friend.

*

"Before we go around pulling up walls, we should pause and reflect long enough on why they were placed there in the first place."

*

Never lose the ability or appreciation to laugh.

*

All tests are not made equally.

*

1) "Blessed is the man that walketh not in the counsel of the ungodly, nor standeth in the way of sinners, nor sitteth in the seat of the scornful. But his delight is in the law of the LORD; and in his law doth he meditate day and night. And he shall be like a tree planted by the rivers of water, that bringeth forth his fruit in his season; his leaf also shall not wither; and whatsoever he doeth shall prosper. The ungodly are not so: but are like the chaff which the wind driveth away. Therefore the ungodly shall not stand in the judgment, nor sinners in the congregation of the righteous. For the LORD knoweth the way of the righteous: but the way of the ungodly shall perish."
- Psalm 1 King James Version (KJV)

*

Life does not stop just because we may experience a setback or obstacle.

*

Remain an open and receptive vessel. Even when
we know, if someone is offering advice, listen.
We should hear what is being presented and
show that we are receptive to guidance.
Do not shut down a giving sharing energy. This is where
knowledge is exchanged, and opportunity is born.

*

9) "After this manner therefore pray ye: Our Father which art
in heaven, Hallowed be thy name. Thy kingdom come, Thy will
be done in earth, as it is in heaven. Give us this day our daily
bread. And forgive us our debts, as we forgive our debtors. And
lead us not into temptation, but deliver us from evil: For thine
is the kingdom, and the power, and the glory, for ever. Amen."
~ Matthew 6:9-13 King James Version (KJV)

*

Do not mishandle the time allotted to
prepare for the next opportunity.

*

Be pragmatic with resources. Being careful
to balance wants versus necessities.

*

We must learn to allow journeys and experiences
to play out. Do not press for resolution
prematurely. Lessons cannot be forced or rushed.

*

As we grow and evolve and share, there will be some that we try
to aid who will choose not to rise above and be more. There will
be some who will speak and act negatively towards you because
of this. Because we continue to grow and evolve, and their lack
of drive causes them to stay. We must not take this personally.

*

Is it more important to you to prove you
are right or know you are right?

*

We must learn to forgive the offence we have
received from others even when they have not
offered an apology or asked for forgiveness.
We cannot carry around their energy and
attachment, allowing it to fester and consume.
We must release it and let it go.
Freeing ourselves of the weight.

*

We are never too inadequate to receive
YAHWEHS love and grace.

*

Imagination Manifestation.

*

When we maximize, those energies and factors
working on our behalf can maximize as well.

*

"When I look back on my life, I overpaid for my big successes
every time. And when I tried to get a bargain, get it a
little cheaper or get a better deal on it, I ended up usually
either getting it and not happy I got it or missing it."
– Jerry Jones

*

"At the banquet table of nature, there are no reserved
seats. You get what you can take, and you keep what you
can hold. If you can't take anything you won't get anything,
and if you can't hold anything, you won't keep anything.
And you can't take anything without organization."
-A. Phillip Randolph

*

We must place ourselves in the environments that

speak to and call to our heart and soul. And

what or who is meant for us will find their

way to us. It is on us to show up.

*

"There can be no community without self-sufficiency."
-Lupe Fiasco

*

"Leaders are like eagles, they don't flock.
You find them one at a time."

*

Do not get too high on wins and too low
on losses. Life is about balance.

*

"That strong mother doesn't tell her cub, son, stay

weak so the wolves can get you. She says,

toughen up, this is reality we are living in."
-Lauryn Hill

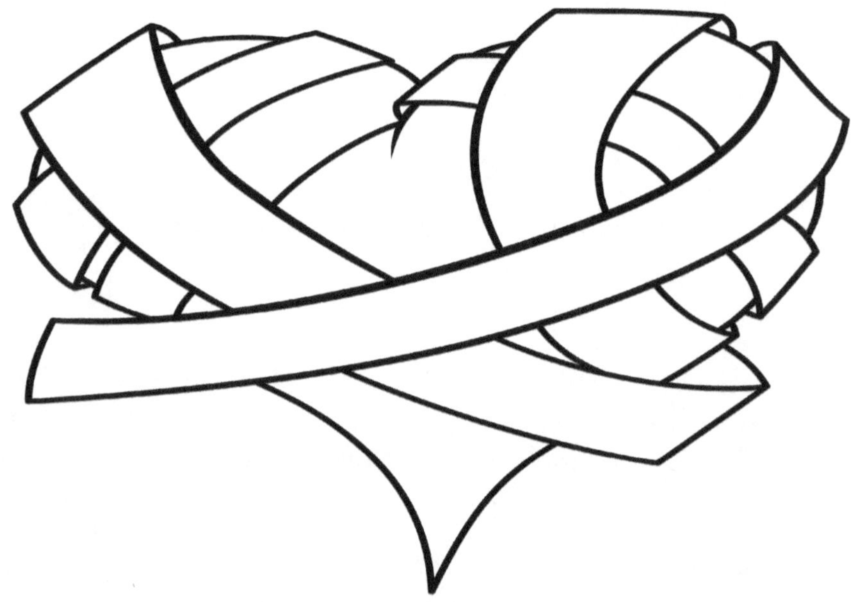

LoveRespectHeal

www.ingramcontent.com/pod-product-compliance
Lightning Source LLC
Chambersburg PA
CBHW031136250726
48655CB00002B/693